MW01241362

Published by Senova Media Publishing
24307 Magic Mountain Parkway
Valencia, CA 91355

Printed in the United States of America

ISBN 978-1-4507-8131-2

http://www.senovamedia.com

Contents

Introduction 3

Song-Writing 4
Music Styles 5
Approaches to Song-Writing 9
Anatomy of a Song 13
Song Stuctures 15
Begin Writing a Song 17

Producing 24
What is a Producer? 25
Pre-Production 27

Recording 38
Basics of Engineering and Recording 39
Hardware Basics 41
Microphone Placement 64

Introduction to Digital Audio Workstations (DAWs) 70
PreSonus Studio One 73

Introduction

Dear reader! Get ready to jump knee-deep into songwriting, producing, and recording.

A lil bit about myself so you know who's writing this stuff...

I have been a professional engineer, song-writer, producer, musician, drum-programmer and mixer since 1986. I DO NOT say that to brag in any way, but to let you know that i've seen a whole lot of "STUFF" and been through a whole lot of STUFF. So everything I write about in here comes from actual application.

I was never the quickest learner in class...it sometimes took me a bit longer to absorb difficult concepts, but once it did click with me, I would zoom past the crowd, kinda like a horse race where one horse starts out the gate last, but by the end of the race was at the head of the pack.

I say all this to explain to you how I like to explain things. I wished people had explained difficult concepts in a simple way when I was coming up. Lots of times, people like to show how smart they are by using fancy terminology. To me, the simpler you can explain something, the better, so that is how I attempted to write this info.

If it seems to get confusing while reading at times, just keep reading because i usually come back to the main point after taking a left turn explaining a side concept.

The three subjects are:

1. *Song-writing*
2. *Producing*
3. *Recording*

Thanks for checking it out!

Song-Writing

PART ONE

These days there are so many different styles of music. In my opinion, it is important to have an understanding of the main, popular styles. Let's list some of them.

1) Pop
2) Rock
3) Urban - R&B
4) Dance/Electronica
5) Metal
6) Rap & Hip Hop
7) Pop-Country

Let's go into each one of these a bit. As you'll see, each of these styles branch off into many smaller groups. (This is the beauty of music - it is difficult to put certain labels on it because producers and songwriters are always creating new styles. Each generation influences the next one).

POP
Wow. Where do I start? Ha ha. The term "pop" is short for the word, "popular," so whatever song reaches the widest variety of listeners is basically considered, "pop-music." Pop can incorporate all types of styles from rap to dance, hard-rock to urban.

The songs from the whole list that have become really popular - songs you might hear in a grocery store or elevator are songs that have "crossed-over" into the Pop category.

ROCK
Rock branches off into smaller groups such as:

- Hard rock
- Indi-rock
- Pop rock
- Corporate rock, etc.

Usually when you think of rock you think of a band - a real drummer playing real drums, a bass and guitar player playing instruments swinging low, distortion on the guitar and an overall aggressive sound. (A member of the band usually begins writing a new song by introducing a guitar riff or a new melody to the rest of the band members).

URBAN - R&B
When thinking of Urban music there is not a large association with live musicians or a real band playing. This style of music most often uses a lot of programmed beats and synths (synthesizers). Songs are generally written by first programming a beat or track into a computer, a drum-machine or some other form of music software.

DANCE/ELECTRONICA
Dance/Electronica music can be broken down into many smaller divisions such as:

> - *Techno*
> - *Trance*
> - *Drums and Bass*
> - *Jungle*
> - *Garage*
> - *Dub-step*
> - *Glitch*
> - *Trip-hop*
> - *Electro*

This style of music has grown like crazy since the year 2000. Computer music software began to hit the market in a big way during this time. Before the year 2000, hard-drives were still pretty expensive and the information passed between a computer and hard-drive simply was not able to move fast enough.

"Electronica" (electronic music) first appeared in the mid 1970's by groups like "Kraftwork." In writing an "electronica" song, a producer or programmer will either begin with a repeating chorus melody-line with the beat being built around it or by creating the beat first and then writing the song around the beat.

METAL

Metal or, "Heavy-Metal" branches off into a few categories such as:

- *Original metal*
- *Death metal*
- *New metal*
- *Speed metal*

Metal almost always is LOUD and DISTORTED! YEAH!!! Like "rock," metal songs are born by a member of the band introducing a cool "riff" to his band mates. Each person will then create his own part for his particular instrument.

Also sometimes whoever in the band writes the lyrics may come up with a cool melodic singing line and the band fits chords around it.

From my studies, most bands write songs together. (In all styles, there is no one way to approach songwriting. I am giving you examples of how I have seen it done).

Many people credit Ozzy Osborne's first band, "Black Sabbath" for inventing heavy metal.

RAP & HIP HOP

Everyone always asks me to explain the difference between rap and hip hop music. Many different people have many different explanations as to the difference between the two.

You can think of the term, "Hip Hop" as describing an entire way of living.. Rapping, break-dancing, graffiti-art, DJ-ing and all the other stuff that goes along with this how the people who do these things dress, the slang words they use and so on. This all can be thought of as a kind of way of life, a "culture."

"Rapping" is also a part of this way of life. So, in essence, they are one and the same; they mean the same thing. There are however the "True-to Heart" fans and artists who say that "Hip Hop" music is the real deal style that does not make it to the radio and that "Rap" music is the more pop-sounding of the two.

Hip-Hop /Rap music breaks out into different variations as well. You have:

- *East Coast*
- *West Coast*
- *Dirty South*
- *Northern/Great Lakes*
- *Miami*
- *Northern Cali*
- *Southern Cali*

Just like "Electronica," writing a rap/hip-hop song usually begins with making the beat first.

Many times though, rappers, (or "MC's" which means, "Master of Ceremonies,") will write lyrics without hearing any beat and will just store the lyrics in a notebook until he or she comes across the right track or beat.

When I say "track," I mean a beat with musical layers on top. When I say "beat," I am usually referring to the programmed drums with very few musical layers added.

COUNTRY MUSIC
We all know what country music sounds like - or at least we think we do. More so than not we think of someone singing in a twangy, southern accent to a slide guitar.   Someone else might say that it sounds sad all the time … ha ha! These are all stereotypes.

Country music is a traditional style of American music that has undergone many transformations. Traditional country music is a blend of bluegrass, gospel, blues and folk music. Country, like the other types of music so far listed, breaks out into many different forms as well. (To name just a few we have)?

- *Honky tonk*
- *Country rock*
- *Rockabilly*
- *Pop-Country*
- *Country soul, others*

Country music usually has very well written lyrics and singable, catchy mel-

8

odies. Many country songs will begin with the lyrics and melody written first and then the music placed to them.

PART TWO

APPROACHING SONGWRITING

It is important to have at least a basic understanding of all these different styles I feel if you intend to truly go after your dream of having success in your music career.

Many times, we don't know how to begin writing that hit song so I would like to break this down and make some suggestions. Below is a short list of ways to begin:

> *Chordially*
> * Beat-driven
> * Sound-driven
> * Lyrics and/or melodies

1. Starting a song Cordially

When I say this, I mean to start messing around on the guitar or piano. Start by playing a few notes or chords, one after the other until you find some that sounds good.

This small cluster of notes or chords is the "DNA" for your song. Once you feel you have found a few chords you like, keep messing around with them by switching up the order you play them in and how fast or slow it is you play them. Play 'em up high, then down low. After a few hours, you will have figured out the right combination and speed. More on this later.

2. Starting a song by first finding a cool Beat

Usually urban R&B, Rap, Pop and even some Rock begin with first creating a cool beat. The terms "beat" and "track" both really mean the same thing, but to be more specific, a "track" usually refers to a beat with more musical layers on it.

But, even a "beat" sounds really cool by itself. Tracks and beats are created either by a drum machine like the "AKAI-MPC," or in a music software program like, "PROTOOLS," "LOGIC," "GARAGE BAND," "STUDIO-ONE," "REASON," "ABELTON, "FRUITY LOOPS" and others.

Lastly, there is a difference between the word, "BEAT" which is a general, generic term for something that has some kind of rhythm to it, (the way an alarm clock may have a rhythmic pattern to the ring) as opposed to our term, "BEAT" which refers to a cool rhythm we create for a cool singer or rapper.

These kind of "beats" need to have unique, and even odd-sounding elements. This means the snare-drum, kick-drum percussion sounds, bass line each need to sound special.

For example, if you hit a real snare drum it will sound like a snare drum right? Duh…but, if you hit the snare drum in the bathroom while flushing the toilet, this background noise is gonna create a unique sound.

Of course, you will know what's going on but someone who does not know what you did will probably say, "WHOA!!..that sounds different, where did you get that snare from? Can I copy it?" Ha ha..as silly as this example is, that probably would be your friend's comment after hearing this snare sound recorded while flushing the toilet.

So, each drum sound you use in a beat should make the listener say, "I wonder how he found that kick drum, snare drum, etc…"

3. Starting a song by finding a cool SOUND
What I mean by "Sound-driven" is if you were to scroll through all of the sounds in a keyboard, you will obviously stumble across a few sounds that really catch your ear because the sound itself sounds spooky, sad, mad, excited, loving or evokes other emotions.

For example: The sound of a deep church bell in the distance might make one person feel warm because it reminds them of going to Church on Sunday with family, where another person might find the sound scary like an old Dracula movie. The point is that the sound of the note itself tells an entire story without even actually playing a bunch of chords.

Now that anyone with a DAW (digital-studio-workstation) like ProTools,

Logic, Reason, Nuendo, Fl-Studio, Abelton or Studio-One has access to virtual synthesizers built right into the program, their chances of finding stimulating, interesting sounds is that much easier. It just takes a little time to be patient and sift through the multitude of sounds in each of these programs.

Once you have found a really cool sound, see how it makes you feel. What emotion does it spark in you? Anger, love, humor, fear? If you are able to identify an emotion, you are half way there. More on this later as well.

4. Beginning a Song by having LYRICS AND/OR MELODIES first

Many songs are born from lyrics and/or melodies. Country music is driven by story telling which mean many country songs begin with lyrics.

Just to be clear, one song-writer may start by humming a "melody" without any words (lyrics) knowing that if he perfects the melody in his head, the lyrics will come.

Another writer may have a catchy phrase without any melody knowing that a melody will come as he adds more words to the catchy phrase. A simple phrase like, "All the King's Men" may be bouncing around in your head for a day or two and you do not know how it is it got there! Happens to me all the time. By me unconsciously repeating it in my head, new thought like, "Who are the King's men," "What do they look like?" "How many are out there?" are born.

Sometimes I have trouble getting my brain to think of something else! Ha So, if you are an obsessive person who tends to focus on things without even trying, you are blessed with a great gift. If I consciously plant an idea in my head, my brain will automatically "go to work" on it as I go about my day. When I revisit the idea in my head later, my brain always produces results. Magically, I have new ideas whenever I do this. You can do this too! It works! Sounds crazy huh? I dare you to try it.

Once someone has a few strong phrases strung together and a melody worked out, cords can easily be put to them. Any decent musician can find the right chords to accompany the lyrics/melodies.

Lastly, I want to stress that there is a difference between lyrics and prose/poetry. I run across many people who write poetry who think their poems can

11

become lyrics to a song. Poetry tends to be bit more intricate and wordier than lyrics. Poetry is usually read by itself whereas lyrics must work well with the music both melodically and rhythmically.

The musical style of "spoken word" is where poetry is read over live music. The poet is free to ebb and flow above the music and both poet and band feed off of each other. For example, if the poet gets loud in a section, the band may grow in intensity behind him/her and vice versa.

In a song, the lyrics have been groomed to blend with the music as if it were an instrument. Lyrics are much more synchronized with the music as to spoken word being much more loose.

What to write about?
Good question. A good place to start is by asking yourself a simple question: What significant things have happened in your life during the past three to six months? Did someone have a baby? Did you win some money? Did you fall in or out of love, see a good movie, read a really great book that sparked your thinking in any way? If you asked yourself and really think about it, many song subjects will pop up.

Let's put songwriting into two subject categories:

> -trendy
> -timeless

Trendy lyrics usually use hip hop slang words or reflect something maybe happening now in the world like a popular person who gets in trouble or use a slang phrase like, "swagger" (cool style) or whatever. These types of songs usually get popular fast then fade after a month or even a few weeks.

Timeless songs tend to speak of more universal themes like love, religion, drama, emotions, etc. This way a date cannot be put on them. It does not matter whether you hear a timeless song today or twenty years from now, the song will always stay relevant because there will always be central themes like love and emotion, etc.

On another note, speaking of trendy or timeless - even if your lyrics are totally timeless, the actual sounds you use for instruments can "date" your song. We all know what "80's" music sounds like:

- *very artificial sounding drums*
- *lots of echo and reverb*
- *kinda nerdy-sounding*
- *cheap-sounding keyboards (haaa)!*

Using sounds that are known for a time-period may put your song in a category you may not want to be in, so remember that.

PART THREE

ANATOMY OF A SONG
Here we are gonna discuss many various sections used in songs Just as a car is made up of many different parts: wheels, engine, frame, dashboard - songs contain many different combinations of parts:

Intro
Pretty simple - the beginning of the song. The intro usually has less music layers than other parts of the song, or is really huge in order to shock the listener and get his attention.

Intros sometimes have lyrics without music, music without lyrics, music and lyrics, music and melodies only or any other way one can think of how to start a song that will capture the listener's attention. Again, sometimes choruses act as intros where the song will begin with the chorus and then go into verse one.

Chorus
Central idea of the story of the song; memorable melody.

Verse
Tells a chapter of the story. Usually songs have two to three verses.

B-section or Pre-Chorus
Usually comes between the verses and choruses; connects verses and choruses together.

Bridge

Many times the bridge comes after the second chorus. The first verse lays out a chapter of our story, then the chorus/hook comes in and paraphrases the story into a catchy phrase. Then the second verse comes back in with another episode or chapter of the story - then maybe a b-section, then the second chorus sums it up again.

Then, the bridge comes in and states how we intend to "fix' the problem we have been expressing in the verses and choruses - what change we intend to make to make things even better for us. (Unclear sentence here..)

Tag

This is a slang word for the section that may come right after the chorus. It is like another small chorus. It usually works great as ear-candy, meaning it is like getting two sweet "hook" actions back to back - double-dipping.

Vamp/Outro

Vamp is another slang term that usually refers to the very end of the song. Vamps grow the song with even more intensity by bringing in more background vocals, bringing in more instruments, transposing the song (raising the entire song by a note or a few for dramatic effect) or any other way to add more intensity to the end of the song.

Gospel songs are very good examples of this in how they may speed up at the very end and send the crowd into a frenzy. Vamps always work, but don't use them too often. I'd say on one song per every five.
Having vamps on too many songs will diminish the overall effect intended. It will start to sound gimmicky and too formulated.

Solo

Duh! We all know what this is. Solos are to showcase a particular instrument in a section with a fancy or simple display of talent. Also, solos are great for either reinforcing the chorus/hook melody, or for introducing a new, catchy melody.

Breakdown

A breakdown is where all of the music drops out and only the beat is heard. Sometimes one instrument is left in with the beat. Breakdowns are great for creating contrast so when the music does come back, it sounds huge.

To make it clear, a chorus and a hook really mean the same thing though they may have other meanings as well. The word chorus usually refers to the overall chorus section, where the term, "hook" can sometimes mean the one line in the chorus that is the most memorable part of the chorus - the line "everyone knows."...

For example, in the song, "I Try" by Macy Gray, the chorus is:

> 1) *"I try and say good-bye and not choke*
> 2) *Try and walk away and I stumble*
> 3) *Though I try to hide it, it's clear*
> 4) *My world crumbles when you are not near"*

In this example, the first and fourth lines are both the hook lines. If you were to sing either of these lines to someone, they will most likely recognize what song you are singing.

SONG STRUCTURES

There is no right or wrong when it comes to song structures. The thing is that usually popular songs have pretty simple song structures.

When I say "song-structure," I mean the order in which you put these individual parts one after the other (verse, chorus, bridge, etc.),

Let's take a look at some typical song structures. Remember, there is no right or wrong way to structure a song, but usually the simpler it is, the more chance you have of reaching a bigger audience.

Key:

C	=	chorus
V	=	verse
B	=	B-sect/pre-chorus
BR	=	bridge
T	=	tag
VP	=	vamp/outro

15

I	=	intro
S	=	solo
BD	=	breakdown

Structure 1
I - V1 - C1 - V2 - C2 - BR - C3 - End

Structure 2
C-Intro - V1 - B1 - C1 - V2 - B2 - C2 BD - BR - C3 - VP

Structure 3
V1 - C1 - Tag - V2 - B - C2 - Tag - V3 - BR - Tag - VP

There are an unlimited amount of variations of song-structures. This is what makes songwriting so fun and challenging! These are just three of at least ten million possibilities with Structure 1 being probably one of the more basic structures.

Structure #2 is popular as well and three is a bit more sophisticated.

In addition to the different sections of a song, each section has a certain length to it. We count section length in terms of "bars."

Most of you folks reading this probably know what a bar is, but for those of you who are not familiar, no problem! Trust me, it is essential you understand bars and beats.

One BAR is equal to 4 taps.

So to count bars, you'd say: "One, two, three, four, two, two, three, four, three, two, three, four, four, two, three, four, five, two, three, four", etc...
we just counted 5 bars.

In contemporary music, most sections are either 4 or 8 bars each. This allows the listener to follow without too many complex turns and changes as in jazz or classical music where there can be many different bar combinations.

PART FOUR

LET'S BEGIN WRITING A SONG

Now that we understand some basics regarding how songs are put together, let's take a stab at writing a song. It really helps to remember "PART 2" of this chapter entitled, "Approaching Songwriting." I laid out four different ways to spark the writing of a song:

1) **Chord driven** - Have you been messing around with a few chords on the guitar or piano?

2) **Beat driven** - Have you been tinkering with a beat?

3) **Sound driven** - have you stumbled upon a killer sound in a synth on your computer?

4) Lyric/Melody driven - Do you or your partner have some lyrics brewin'? A cool story to tell?

Whichever of these you may have, start there! When being creative, it is always best to jump right into it and to NOT "think" about it too much. Too much thinking will usually slow you down. There is an old phrase that fits in perfect here: "The paralysis of analysis." This means that there is too much thinking and not enough action!

Once you have created one of these four sparks, open up a "click-track" in your computer music program (studio-one, garage-band, logic, protocols, reason, fl-studio) and "document" the idea.

When I say "document" the idea, I mean to record what you have as-it-is. It is okay if it is not fully though out (few chords, rough beat, cool synth sound or lyric/melody idea). The important thing is to lay it down in a "session" so you can begin to think of other parts to add to build the song out.

*IF YOU DO NOT have any of these four sparks already going, it is time to get one going! Here are some tips on how to get this ball moving.:

1) Grab a guitar or get a keyboard and just start fiddling. It is sometimes helpful to randomly skip through the radio dial for a few minutes or ran-

domly turn your I-tunes on to get your creative juices going. I DO NOT mean copy someone else's music! I mean literally to scroll through some stations quickly just to tickle your ears and brain.

2) Scroll through some drum-loops. See if there is a groove that moves you. Don't think about each loop too much, just scroll through a library of loops and whichever ones get you thinking right-away, drag these into your session and build bass, guitar, keyboard parts to the loop.

If you do not play an instrument, find a buddy who does and feed him ideas of what you want him to play to the loop.

> A) Play something heavy and mean.
> 2) Play something light and happy.
> 2) Play something jazzy.
> 4) Play something with lots of rhythm.

You will be surprised at what you pull out creatively from him if you give out a few directions. (This is what a producer does).

3) Get on a cool synthesizer, or open a "VST" (virtual-synthesis-technology) keyboard in your DAW (digital-audio-workstation: Studio-one, Reason, Logic, Protocols, etc.). You do not need to be a keyboardist to simply scroll through the sounds in these synthesizers.

Just like the drum loops, scroll through the synth sounds until you find one that touches you - evokes a mood for you. Again, don't think to much! Just listen and feel.

"A great sound will inspire an entire song."

4) If you have a melody only, try to find a few chords that go along with the melody. It is always cool to write with another person or even a few other people. You will be surprised at how many ideas will be sparked.

If you have lyrics only, try saying the lyrics over and over in a rhythmic way. Eventually, you will get a feel for how the rhythm of the lyrics should sound. Once this happens, melodies will begin to present themselves automatically, especially if you are bouncing your ideas off of others in the room with you.

If you start out with both lyrics and melodies, it will be even that much easier to put them to music. If you don't feel you have the best ear in finding chords on guitar or piano, then collaborate with someone who does. Again, you will be so surprised at how easily ideas begin to flow! Once this happens you will be hooked forever.

"Document" initial element to "scratch" track:
When I say to "document" something, I mean to record it. Instead of focusing on the very best way to record it, I mean to do it without much thought. Kind of like drawing a pencil sketch of something. You are not going for accuracy - you are just getting the preliminary idea across.

Once you feel you have either:

> *1) Some cool chords worked out*
> *2) A cool drum-beat going*
> *3) Have found a great synth sound*
> *4) Have the beginnings of some great lyrics and/or melody*

Then - open up a new "session" in your "DAW" (described at the beginning of this book) and put your idea down. (Record it)!

Even though you might not have the whole thing worked out, still go ahead and record your idea.

Continue to write song to completion:
Writing with others is a great way to build your song out and find new ideas you never thought of. I strongly suggest everyone try it! You might have to try out a few different people before you find ones you really enjoy writing with.

If you are a "music-writer," meaning, you write the chords or make the beat, then you will wanna find a good lyricist. You may also wanna work with other "chord" people as well. As I said, you'll be surprised at what you come up with creatively when you collaborate with others.

How to proceed with co-writers:
Play what you have so far for the co-writer even if it is far from complete. If you have an idea of what is missing from your song, tell the co-writer what you are thinking of, but allow the co-write to be creative and do his "own-thing."

Try not to be a dictator and overly-controlling in what it is they might be hearing for the song. At the same time, if what the co-writer is coming up with is very, very different from where you want the song to go, tell the co-writer that he/she is too far creatively from where you are hearing the song going and try to find happy compromise.

Continue to add musical layers to the initial scratch tracks until the song begins to develop out. Make sure to be a filter though - meaning, don't keep every idea that co-writer comes up with.

"It is okay to not use every idea."

When am I done?
The million dollar question is, "how will I know when the songwriting is complete?"

You are not alone asking this question! A good way is to get away from the song for a few days. Don't listen to the song for a few days. Then when you do listen to it again, you will know in your heart if it is complete or not.

If you are still not sure if it is done, ask a few people who are not attached to the song to listen and see if they think it is done.

But, beware that most people will hear the raw "document" sounds you are playing around with and think that they are the real sounds. They will not be hearing the actual quality of the "song" itself because the "production" (better sounds and parts perfected) have not been done yet.

Once you realize that the raw layers have set a clear enough picture of how the song will sound, you are now done "writing" the song and ready to re-cord the song for real. What I mean by this is now that the chords, the tempo, the lyrics and melodies are all figured out, it is now time to go back and replace the rough sounds used with better sounding and better-played parts.

Also, it is time to have a singer actually give a killer performance and sing the lyrics and melodies down like their life depend on it! The rough vocal ideas you used while figuring it all out does not showcase the lyrics/melodies the way they need to be.

So, the next step between writing the song and actually recording the song for real is to be aware of what a record-producer does. We will dig into this in the next chapter, but first let's finish this songwriting chapter by looking at how to split the ownership of a song between the co-writers.

Splitting ownership of a song:
Trust me, there is no perfect formula as to how to go about splitting up a song! Let's start with some basics.

A traditional way of viewing a song:

> *50% lyrics
> *50% lyrics and melody

Whoever participated in creating the music and/or track gets a piece of the 50% music side." Whoever participated in writing the lyrics (words) and/or the melody gets a piece of the "50% lyrics/melody side.

VERY IMPORTANT NOTE: There is a complete difference between someone who actually thinks up the chords for a song as opposed to a musician you bring in at the end who takes the chords already written and then re-records them for you with killer sounds. This second person is not a "writer" of the song - only a "performer" on the song.

Let's say there are only three chords in the entire song written by Roscoe. Then, Sebastian is asked to come in and make these three chords sound cool. So, Sebastian comes in with a really dope pedal-board with tons of guitar effects, a great selection of guitars and takes those three chords and makes them sound really incredible.

Even though Sebastian made those three simple chords sound like so much more - he is not a "writer," but only a performer on the song.

Writer - *gets a piece of ownership of song (copyright).*

Performer - gets paid at a session for his playing and gets a credit on the record - "guitar by…"

Performer does not get any "royalties." Only the writer gets royalties.

What is a royalty?

A royalty is a payment to someone who owns a piece, or all of a song (a writer) when the song is sold on a record or is played on the radio or TV…in essence when the song is transacted in some way commercially.

A payment may come from a radio station who pays a songwriter each time the radio station plays the song on the air; it may come from a record label - for example, if Celine Dion sings a song written by you and puts it one her album, really, she is just renting the song from you so every time she sells a record with your song on it, she (her label) has to pay you some rent which is otherwise known as a royalty.

What is a Copyright?

A copyright is just a fancy word which also means who it is that owns/controls the use of a song.

A common mistake most people make is thinking that the copyright office (Library of Congress in D.C.) issues copyrights. Not true!

The copyright office in Washington D.C. only offers "Copyright-protection." They are really just like a witness of something you are claiming is yours.

Here is an example - let's say you have some lyrics and a cool melody in your head. You sing them for people and they love 'em. But, you have not recorded them yet.

Once you record the lyrics and melody, you actually "own" that recording, correct? Correct! Since you own the "rights to that one copy," you now own the "copy-right." It is that simple. You have total control over who you let make copies/duplicates of that original recording.

BUT!!!! Let's say someone hears your original recording and takes the idea and creates their own version of your lyrics and melodies? Well, if you have not protected the idea by having someone else witness you created it on a given day, then that person can claim it is theirs.

So before you let anyone hear the recording, you want to protect yourself to prove you came up with the idea first. The way you prove this is by having a witness/entity listen to it first before anyone else so you can always call on them to confirm the day you let them hear the original.

This is what the Library of Congress/Copyright office in Washington D.C. does - they issue "copyright protection." They are witness that you created the idea first.

Producing

PART ONE

What exactly does a record producer do?

A producer has many jobs in producing a music project. A few of the most important roles are:

1) Knowing how to do "pre-production" really well.
2) Knowing how to identify sounds.
3) Know how to motivate musicians and singers to perform their very best when recording their parts on a song.

In a nut shell, a producer must know how to organize and motivate people. Let's go through these three points in more detail.

Pre-production - what the heck is it?

"Pre" means before
"Production" means recording for real.

What I mean when I say "recording for real" is when I am writing the song, I am not necessarily focused on how good the actual sound of my guitar is or how well I play the chords. I am more focused on figuring out the chords and creating the best song possible. After the song is written (rough recording of the song like a pencil sketch), it is then time to re-record/re-place the pencil-sketch sounds with really cool sounds and play those parts really well).

So, back to pre-production. As I said, it means "before" we "record" so we must make sure the song is the best it can be and also we must get a plan as to how to best go about recording the record. For example:

A) Are we gonna add live drums if the song was initiated with a drum-loop from a machine?

B) Are we gonna record all of the musicians at the same time or one at a time?

C) Which musicians will do the best job? Do we need to scout around let's say for a guitarist who has a certain playing style or who has a huge pedal board of efx?

D) Are we gonna have the drummer play to a "click-track" so that he stays in time better or let him play free which will give the song a more "live" feel?

E) Can our drummer even play to a click-track?!! Ha ha. (It is not the easiest thing to do well.)

F) What studio are we gonna use? Are we gonna record the drums at a bigger studio where we can use more microphones, then go back to our home studio and record all of the other elements/instruments one at a time?

There are so many options to think about but I don't want it to sound too complicated. It really comes down to some basic, common sense decisions.

If you just take a moment and think each song through, the best plan will come to you.

Just think about the overall "sound" you want the song to have. Think of a song by a band you like and use that song's sound as a "reference" for the way you want your song to sound like.

I don't mean copy the same chords!! I mean think of the overall "mood" the song has. Are the guitars smooth and polished sounding or are they ratty like punk-rock? Are the drums big as if they are being played in a stadium, or do they have no echo to them and sound tight and dry as if played in a padded closet?

Think of how you want each element (instrument) in your production to sound and how you want it played by the musician. Once you know the overall "sound" of the song you want, then just pick each instrument apart in your head and think how it should sound for the song.

This goes for the vocals as well. Do you want the vocals to sound raw and aggressive like punk-rock or gansta-rap or smooth and polished like "RnB" dance music with lots of background vocals coming in and out around the lead vocal?

It is your job as the producer to let the singer know how you want him or her to sing the lead vocal and whether you want him/her to do background vocals or not. If so, then help them come up with background parts.

PART TWO

So how do we get started with pre-production?

Now that we've touched base overall on how the producer must have an overall vision of the song/songs, let's begin the actual process.

The first is "critical-listening." When I say this, I mean it is time for you to first make sure the song itself is the best it can be before we jump into thinking of the overall sound of each instrument. Critical-listening means that you try to tear the song apart to see if it stands up - kind of like car companies doing crash tests to see how durable their product is before they paint it and make it look all fancy.

How to do this? - Good question!! Simple answer We need to pick the song apart. Let's list five ways to pick a song apart:

> *1) Lyrics*
> *2) Melody*
> *3) Structure*
> *4) Tempo*
> *5) Key of Song*

1) Lyrics

The good news is that as a producer, I don't really need to fix anyone's lyrics. I just need to point out to the writer when the lyrics are bad. Remember, creativity is purely subjective - meaning that there is no right or wrong. Everyone has an opinion when it comes to creativity.

Still however, in my opinion there are a couple things that usually make lyrics bad:

> ** Too many cliché's*
> ** Too "wordy."*

What is a cliché?

A cliché generally is a phrase we have heard before like, "A penny for your thoughts," "The whole kit-n-kaboodle," or, "A penny saved is a penny earned."

In lyric writing, when I say "cliché," I am referring to overly used phrases and also phrases that are just too easy to think up. I call these, "throw away" lyrics. For example, I was working with an artist who wrote this hook:

> *"I know all your true colors*
> *Yellow, green, black and white*
> *I know all your true colors*
> *Yeah, that's right."*

I challenged the artist to come up with another last line because it was a "throw away" lyric. She came up with this:

> *"I know your true colors*
> *Yellow, green, black and white*
> *I know all your true colors*
> *Like the back of my hand, that's no lie..."*

The new line, "Like the back of my hand, that's no lie," I felt was so much better than what she had prior because if you know someone as well as you know the "back of your hand," then you are really telling the listener something important instead of just throwing out some generic line that rhymes like, "yeah, that's right."

In conclusion, it is important to state that many hit songs use cliché's here and there. They can be a real effective tool for creating catchy hooks, but be aware of two things regarding cliché's:

> *A) Too many cliché's strung together*
> *B) "Throw away" lines*

What is "wordiness"?
Have you ever heard someone's lyrics that sound more like a Shakespeare sonnet than song lyrics?... There is a difference between poetry and song-lyrics. Here is an example of wordiness:

"The lightening in the sky reminds me of the eloquence of your heart, because when you share your feelings, it sets off a spark that says that my love shows the impression of desert sands."

Oh my God- how obnoxious! The words just go on and on and on but at the end you really don't even know what it is that is being talked about.

In my opinion, the best lyrics are pretty straight-ahead in their meaning - conversational as if the singer is telling you a story at dinner. It is interesting, but not confusing.

2) Melody
The second way to pick a song apart is by seeing if the song has any melodies that the listener will remember. A memorable melody is so so so important! A good example of a memorable melody is the "Birthday Song." You cannot forget this melody even if you tried…!!

If the style of music you are working on is RAP, or something like Death-metal where the singer is screaming, then it is important that the music contain some musical-hooks instead of the vocals.

3) Structure
The third way to pick apart a song is by its structure. When I say structure, I mean two things:

> A) *The order of the sections of the song*
> B) *How long the song is overall.*

For example, if a certain section of a song - let's say the verse, repeats itself over and over one after another before moving on to the next section, the listener is probably gonna get bored hearing that section over and over. We as people like variety whether it is food, movies, conversations, etc. We usually don't like it when things stay the same for too long. Well, the same goes for listening to a song.

My general rule is: The shorter the better when it comes to songs. Remember, the listener usually has a very short attention-span, especially when they are not familiar with the song. It is usually better to surprise the listener and make the song shorter rather then take the chance of boring a listener with a song that is too long.

So, as a critical-listener, see if you think any section of the song takes too long to get through. Simply listen to the song as if it were your first time hearing it and see if you get bored with any of the sections in the song. If you do, maybe you can suggest to the writer or the artist that that section maybe should be cut in half, or made to be more exciting in some way.

4) Tempo

The fourth way to analyze a song is to see if the tempo/speed is right for the song. When I say, "tempo" I am referring to the beats-per-minute (BPM) of the song. This is the way we measure the speed - just like we measure temperature in "degrees" - (95 degrees = hot)

To give you an idea of general BPM's of different styles of music, here is a basic chart:

60-70 BPM	ballad/love song
75-90 BPM	classic rock...ala Led Zepplin
95-105 BPM	R&B/Urban music..."Ludacris"
115-140 BPM	"electro" dance music
150-180 BPM	"Drum & Bass" electronica music

Remember when we first documented the song idea in the beginning, we were not clear what the idea would blossom into? We were not focused on capturing the exact right tempo, we just wanted to get the idea down first.

Now that the idea has grown into the beginnings of a really cool song, it is important that we now go back and get all of the details right, like the tempo.

Making sure the tempo is right for the song is not necessarily the easiest thing to do - meaning knowing if the rough version of the song is moving too fast or too slow does not just jump out at everyone. It takes a bit of concentration to figure out whether the tempo is right or not.

Sometimes the tempo of the rough idea is good...other times the rough idea may seem to "drag" a bit. When I say drag I mean the tempo should speed up a bit because it sounds boring.

Other times if you have a song that has a cool dance groove to it, you may need to slow it down a bit to let the grove "swing" more.

So, in conclusion, determine whether the song is a dance groove song, or is it supposed to be a head-banger song. If you start here, this will give you a good idea whether you have a good tempo or not. If it is not the right tempo, try having the drummer play to a click track at a faster or slower tempo when you re-record the song for real.

5) Key of Song
The fifth and last way to pick a song apart to see if it is a great idea or not is to see whether the key of the song is either too high or too low. Remember, when we were first writing the song. We were not clear where the song idea would go - we were just being creative. But, now that the song has taken shape by us adding layers and writing new sections, it is now time to look/listen to the song and see exactly what it is we have created so far. It is like a painter. He paint and paints, but eventually he steps back from painting and sees if anything is missing.

Back to the "key." This is pretty easy to figure out whether the key is too high or low. Just listen to the lead vocal. If the singer has too much trouble reaching notes throughout the song, then you may wanna try playing the song a few notes down so the singer can hit those notes easier.

If the song is too low then the opposite happens. Usually this pertains to female singers. Some times the song is too low for the girl singer to hit many notes and she is not able to sing with any power. Play the song a few notes higher so she is more in her comfort range of singing.

ARE YOU WORKING WITH A BAND OR A SOLO ARTIST?
Now that you have picked the song apart by analyzing lyrics, melody, structure, tempo and key and have figured out some ways to make the song better, it is now time to think about how you are gonna go about actually recording the song over "for real."

As I mentioned earlier, first writing the song is only the rough draft. After you write it, then you need to re-record it for real using:

-better sounding instruments
-better played parts

- a great vocal performance and background vocals (if need be)
- incorporating the ideas you discovered on how to make the lyrics/
* Melodies/structure/tempo and key better in the song.*

One of the first things you think about is whether this song is intended for a band, or a solo artist.

LET'S TAKE A LOOK AT THESE FOR A SECOND:

BAND
Here are some steps on how to get a band ready to record the song for real in the studio.

Take the Band into a Rehearsal Hall
Before you go into the studio, rent a cheap rehearsal hall or set up in someone's garage and get the band to be able to play the song incorporating all of the new ideas on how to make it better. I like to break down the rehearsal schedule in four steps like this:

A) Have band rehearse song with the new tempo (using a metronome-drummer puts earpiece in), new song-structure if any and new key if changed.

B) Next, have drummer and bass player play together only to make sure drummer's kick-drum pattern is in sync with bass-player's pattern.

C) Create cool parts for each instrument/member. For example, the guitar player might be just playing the same rhythm over and over throughout the song. Maybe suggest to him to play arpeggios in one section instead of just "chunking" hard in every section.

This goes for any musician/band member you feel is just playing the same exact way all the way from the beginning of the song 'till the end...booooor-ing!!!!!!

D) Lastly, now that you have some new ways to play the different sections of the song, make sure the band can play the entire song from top to bottom smoothly without messing up. Have the band rehearse the song over and over will make it feel more natural to them.

So, when you finally do go into the RECORDING studio with the band, they will be able to perform the song well by being able to put their heart and soul into their parts without having to think too hard.

If someone is thinking about his part too much in the studio, he is not gonna play his part as well because it will not feel like second nature to him. Same goes for a band playing a gig.

You can always tell whether a band has rehearsed enough or not. If they have not rehearsed enough, they will be looking at each other on stage with puzzled expressions on their faces. Obviously, they are not giving their best performance to the audience! The same goes for going into the recording studio. The puzzled looks should be figured out in the rehearsals prior to going into the studio. The recording studio is where they should be giving their very best performance.

SOLO ARTIST
When I say "solo-artist," I mean someone who does not have a band. Let's break this term down into two categories:

A) Singer/songwriter
John Mayer, Allanis Morrisette, Macy Gray - these artists write their own songs, but usually did not have a band when they first started. John Mayer could play his songs on guitar, but did not have a band when he first got signed. A record-producer helped him add the layers to his songs to create the cool, organized sound of his first record.

B) Performing-artist
Beyonce, Brittney Spears, Celine Dion, Janet Jackson, Diana Ross and Frank Sinatra - all of these artists fall under this category. These artists do not write their own songs. They sing songs written by producers and song-writers and rely on their producer to create their "sound," meaning help them determine whether their music will sound dancy, hard-rock, R&Bish, or whatever. These performing artists are known for their vocal style, look and personality as opposed to singer-songwriters who are also known for the lyrics they write and the stories they tell.

So, back to whether you are working with a band or a solo-artist. If working with a band, you are most likely gonna take the band into a rehearsal studio and get them to practice playing the song tight before going into the recording studio to record the song for real. But since a "solo-artist" does not have a band, most likely gonna work on the song in your "DAW," (Protools, studio-1. Logic, cubase, etc).

There is no need to rent a rehearsal studio since the solo artist has no band. But, regardless of if you are working with a band or a "solo-artist," the song still comes first. This means that we need to either write or find a song for the solo-artist to sing that will represent his or her musical direction. Once you find or write a song, then it is time to pick the song apart using the five categories:

1) *Lyric*
2) *Melody*
3) *Structure*
4) *Tempo*
5) *Key*

You need to tweak and cater the song to the solo artist so it fits just right for them. If you don't analyze the song using these steps, you will miss the opportunity to make the song the best it can be for that particular artist. It is a way of customizing the song for the artist.

After tweaking and customizing the song for the solo-artist, it is now time to determine the best way to go about recording the song "for real," for the artist. Here are just a few different ways you could do this:

A) Re-create all the music in the "DAW" using hand-picked internal sounds.

B) Record real drums, then add all the other sounds using internal keyboards from the "DAW."

C) Create drums in the "DAW," then record live musicians to create the various layers of the production.

D) Use all live musicians to re-create the song. This way, you (producer) need to guide each musician as to how you want them to play each part.

Remember, this is not a band who have their own ideas. You are "hiring" these musicians to come in and play how you want the song to turn out in the end.

There are many, many different ways to approach laying the song down for the solo-artist. If you visualize how you want the song to sound when it's all done, it will help you determine how to go about doing each layer you record.

Be open to finding songs out there by famous bands and artists you like and use their sound as a reference for how you want your production to sound.

Listen to each instrument, each vocal layer and try to figure out how they did it. This is a huge help in understanding building out the layers in your song.

RECORDING THE SONG "FOR REAL":

After the song is written and after the "pre-production" process of tearing the song apart by analyzing lyrics, melody, song-structure, tempo and key and after the band is taken into a rehearsal space and the song has been practiced with all the new changes, or, after you've figuring out how the song should sound for the solo-artist, it is then time to actually record the song for real.

When you begin this process, the focus should be on two things primarily:

A) Getting the best performances out of each musician and singer who plays on the final version.

B) Getting their best sounds for each layer you add to the song.

Let's go into each of these in more detail. In terms of musicians and singers who perform on your production/song, it is the producer's job to first let each performer know what is expected of them playing-wise, then motivate each player into giving the best performance they can.

From my experiences producing, most musicians truly want to do their best but usually need some coaching to really get there.

Before we begin recording their part, I'll give the musician a general idea of how it is I want them to play the part and I will of course let them hear the original scratch idea created when writing the song.

I might tell the musician:

- *"Give me something mean and loud."...or*

- *"Play the chords soft with distortion."...or*

- *"Play the part so it sounds like aliens are playing it, etc."*

This will put the musician in a certain frame of mind and will open up their creativity.

As they play it down a few times, they will probably begin to get a better feel for it. Let them play with it a few times before you start giving them too many comments on how to do it better. If you don't give them a chance to get used to it first, the may not be as open to your suggestion next.

If you ever come across a singer or a musician unwilling to try something you ask them to to try - phrase the question this way, "just indulge me please...I know my idea sounds stupid but just try it for me one time please." Usually most people will try it for you if you are sincere when you phrase it like this.

A lot of producing music is knowing how to "read" people's personalities. Being a music producer is a lot like being a psychologist. You must be flexible and know when to allow a person to act out, or when you need to take control or end the session if you see musicians getting too frustrated or too tired.

Finding the best sounds possible is another thing you as a producer must do. First of all, when I say "best sound," that is a subjective term meaning there is a right or wrong. But, think of yourself as the leader of a safari - it is up to you to explore and find the coolest, most interesting things. The same is for a producer. It is his or her job to be the crazy person and find the best sounds possible.

For example, if a guitar player brings in a cool pedal-board of effects, I will probably make sure he tries out these effects for me to see what cool sounds we come across.

I wil make sure that each musician I bring in will play around with their instrument in as many ways as possible before we record to make sure we have the coolest and most unique sound possible.

Even if they have to play their instrument upside-down!! I want them to mess-around with every button and gadget they bring with them to hear all of the many various sounds they can make. The more sounds they audition for me, the more choices I have in finding the coolest sounds.

Recording

PART ONE

Basics of engineering and recording
The art of recording music has gone through many huge changes since the year 2000. This was the year when recording-in-the-computer started to really take off. Before the year 2000, most pro's were still recording to 2 inch, magnetic tape...those huge reels you see in old photos of studios.

Even though music-recording software has drastically changed how we record music, there are still many techniques that will always stay the same.

These basic recording principles are:
1) Signal-flow:
Moving electricity (sound) from one device to the next, "out" of one device "in" to the next. We will get back to this.

2) Understanding some basic recording tools:
     A) Differences between microphones
     B) Microphone pre-amps
     C) Equalizers
     D) A/D - D/A converters
     E) Compressors...(more on this later too).

3) Microphone placement:
Understanding how to mic-up different instruments such as drums, guitar amps, vocals, basses and anything else. (More on this later).

4) Editing and Mixing:
Editing is knowing how to cut and paste sounds in your DAW and mixing when all songs are finally recorded, it is time to set the levels so the final product sounds great.

How to get music into the box??!
Basically, there are three ways to get music into your DAW.

             1) Record sounds from the real world.
             2) Record "MIDI" information
             3) "Import" pre-recorded sounds from a CD/DVD or hard-drive.

1) Recording Sounds from the real world can mean anything like:
Voices, guitars, basses, drums, keyboards/pianos, marching-bands, DJ-Turn tables, drum machines, thunder - any sound that is created outside of the computer. To record most of these, you need a microphone to turn acoustic sound waves in the air into electrical energy.

So, a microphone is a "transducer" that changes air-pressure into electricity, and on the opposite side, a speaker is a transducer that turns electricity back into acoustic air-pressure.

2) Record MIDI Information:
To record MIDI information you need to hook up a keyboard controller to your computer. (One of those mini keyboards without controls on them) -

First of all, what does MIDI stand for? It stands for Musical-Instrument-Digital-Interface. But, who cares what it stands for as long as you know how to use it! Haaa! MIDI is kind of like those old pianos that play by themselves when you put a "paper-roll" into them.

You first need top hook up a keyboard controller to your computer/DAW by using a MIDI-cable. Next. You need to open a virtual synth in your DAW. This computerized synthesizer is where the sounds are generated.

1) Keyboard controller - sends a MIDI (trigger) signal to a virtual key-board in the computer.
2) Virtual synthesizer - receives MIDI-trigger note and puts a sound on it.

The coolest thing about virtual synths is that most music software programs have many different synths each with tons of incredible sounds in them.

Before the year 2000, you had to buy actual, hard synthesizers that cost thousands of dollars each! Getting access to killer keyboard sounds has become so much easier.

3) "Importing" pre-recorded sounds:
When I say "import," I mean to pull a sound already stored on a DVD, CD or Hard-drive and place it into the new session you are working on now. Kind of like if you are working on a report in the library and you go to grab a book off the shelf for some specific info you need. These books are always

available when you need them.

I personally have a great library of "samples" (recorded-sounds) in my computer ready to be accessed whenever I need. When I say, "samples," I mean unique, crazy sound-bites like:

-crazy vocal phrases
-lightening and thunder
-cool drums and beats
-unique keyboards, bass and guitar lines
-car screeches
-spaceship sounds, and thousands more!

Whenever I come across something that catches my ear, whether it be musical or not, I'll stop and capture the sound and store it on my main harddrive under the heading, "soundbank." A money bank is where you store money and a soundbank is where I store all cool sound-bites on my hard drive. Now, all of these sounds are available to me whenever I am working on something. The coolest thing is that my soundbank grows every time I work because I am always stumbling on new, cool soundbites.

PART TWO

HARDWARE BASICS

Let's go over some of the most commonly used recording gear.

Microphones - To keep it simple, I like to break down mics into 4 groups.

A) Dynamic mics
B) Condenser mics
C) Tube mics

A) Dynamic Mics

Think of these kind of microphones as "un-powered" mics. Dynamic mics have no electricity running through them, unlike condenser and tube mics.

Think of a dynamic (unpowered) mic kind of like a windmill. A windmill needs lots of wind to make to propeller move. A small breeze of wind will not make the propeller move. It is purely "wind-driven."

You can kind of think of a dynamic mic in this same way. It will not pick up a sound unless the sound is aimed right into the mic. If a dynamic mic is not right up on the source of the sound (voice, guitar, amp,etc) it will only pick up a tiny bit of the sound.

So, to sum these examples up, a dynamic mic needs lots of sound going right into the mic for I to work well.

Also, it can take lots of sound without getting damaged, meaning you can put it right up against a guitar amp set on "10" and it will work just fine. This is not the case with condenser and tube mics. Since they have electricity, they are much more sensitive and would get damaged if you put them right up against a lead guitar amp.

Dynamic mics are really good for "isolation" purposes too. What does that mean? If you are miking up a drum kit, you would probably use dynamic mics on the close drums for two reasons:

1) The mics can handle the loud volume of the drums.

2) Each mic will only pick up the drum it is aimed at. This way, you can record the snare, toms, hihat, at the same time and each mic will only pick up the drum that it is on.

B) Condenser Mics
Unlike dynamic mics, condenser mics do have electricity running through them when in use. This power running through the mics makes the mic much more sensitive than an un-powered/dynamic mic.

In the same windmill example from earlier, imagine if the big blades on the windmill had a small motor attached to its shaft to help even soft breezes of wind turn the blades. This way, even the lightest breeze would move the propeller on the windmill. Same goes with condenser mics; they pick up the very faintest of sounds.

The name of the type of electricity you run through condenser mics is called, "phantom power," or "+48volts." (If you wish to understand why it is called "phantom power," or "+48volts" please feel free to look it up on Wikipedia.)

All mic pre-amps generate phantom-power. (We will discuss mic-pre amps in detail in the next section). So, when you connect a condenser mic to a mic preamp using a microphone chord, electricity travels two ways through the mic chord:

> 1) Mic-pre sends phantom power to the mic
> 2) Mic sends vocal to the mic-pre

When you use a dynamic (un-powered) mic, signal only goes from the mic to the mic-pre.

Every mic-pre has a "phantom-power" on/off switch. So, when you use a dynamic mic, you leave "phantom power" off, and with a condenser, you turn "phantom" on.

So, let's compare dynamic and condenser mics so far:

Dynamic Mics

> 1)Less sensitive to soft sounds
>
> 2)Handles very loud sounds
>
> 3) Picks up only what is right in
>   Front of it, so better for
>   isolating sound.
>
> 4)Un-powered mic. Only the
>   wind from your voice or instrument
>   makes magnet move inside mic.
>
> 5) Use on: Snare drum, inside kick
>   Drum, up close on guitar amp
>   screen, vocal mic on stage for
>   Live performance, etc.
>
> 6)Costs: $35 - $200 appx.

7)Popular Models:
Shure sm-57, shure sm-58
AKG D-112 (good for bass
Amps and kick drums),
Sennheiser 421

Condenser Mics

1)More sensitive to soft sounds

2)Do not handle very loud sounds well.

3)Picks up anything and everything in the area.
Since it is more sensitive, sounds cleaner and
clearer than dynamics.

4)Uses electricity called, "Phantom-
Power" to make mic more sensitive.
Even the softest sound will be picked up.

5)Use-on: Recording vocals in an
isolated, sound-proof room - use
as a "room" mic to record drum-kit,
recording acoustic guitar- piano, record
the sound of an audience, etc.

6)Costs : $100 - $3,000 and up.
(You can get a good sounding condenser
mic for a few hundred dollars these days.

7)Popular Models : Neumann u-87,
AKG 414, AKG 451, Blue Bluebird,
MXL-V67g.

Before we move on and talk about the third kind of mic - tube mics, let's discuss a few more things that all microphones have in common.

*Pick-up patterns
*Diaphragm sizes

Pick-up pattern: This is the area the mic will pick up. There are three common pick-up patterns:

1) "cardioid"
2) "Omni"
3) "Figure 8"

1) "Cardioid" - means the mic picks up in front of the mic only. It is named after the root word "Cardiac" which also refers to the heart.

Imagine a Valentine heart. If the mic is put a the bottom point of the heart shape, all that area inside the heart shape is what the mic will pick up best. Anything outside of the heart shape will not be picked up as well as in the heart.

This is the most common position to set the mic to because normally, you only want to pick up what is in front of the microphone.

2) "Omni" - means he mic will pick up anything from any angle. It is represented on the mic as a circle shape.

You would set the mic to this pick-up pattern - for instance, if you had ten people to record at one time. You could ask them to form a circle with their shoulders touching, then you would place the mic right in the center. All ten singers would be picked up by the mic equally.

3) "Figure-8" - means exactly that...the mic will pick up in the shape of a number 8. The number 8 is really one circle stacked on top of another circle.

If you were to place a mic right where the circles meet in the middle, the area inside each circle is what would be most picked up by seting the mic to this pattern.

You may wanna set a mic to the figure-8 position if you, let's say for instance, have two vocalists and they need to look at each other as they record their parts. You would position the vocalists facing each other with the mic directly between them.

Next, let's discuss diaphragm size. A diaphragm is the filament that moves in the mic when sound-waves push up against it. Microphone diaphragms range between three sizes:

Large diaphragm
Regular diaphragm
Small diaphragm (or "pencil")

Why would we use one diaphragm size over another? To answer this, we need to understand sound waves a bit. We can break sound down into three groups:

Treble (Hi-end)
Mid-range
Bass (Low-end)

We can think of sound waves traveling through the air just like ripples moving through water. If you were to drop a pebble in a pond of very still water, you will see the waves begin to radiate out from where the pebble hit the water.

This is how sound waves travel through the air.

If the waves are closer together as they radiate out, your ear will be tickled faster and you will hear a sizzly, hi-pitched sound.

The air-waves are touching your ear quickly one after another...they are hitting your ear more "frequently"...or at a higher "frequency" aha!

On the other hand, if the waves are further apart from one another, your ear will perceive it as a muffled, bassy sound.

So, we can conclude that bass waves are "wider" than trebly, hi-end sounds which are much closer together. When I say wider, I mean there is more

46

empty space between each wave. The waves are reaching your ear less "frequently"...or at a lower "frequency". aha!

Back to the diaphragm size - the bigger the diaphragm, the more bass the mic will pick up. The smaller the diaphragm, the more treble, or hi-end it will pick up.

(Hi-end sounds like sizzle, mid-range sounds like an announcer on a loudspeaker at a stadium - real nasally. Low end sounds like if you taste something good and say, "mmmmmm." to yourself. So, sizzle, nasally and "mmmmm" all work together to make up something that sounds like everyday life. As an engineer, you will need be able to hear each one of these "tones" in everything you hear).

So, to sum up diaphragm size, I would use a large diaphragm mic to pick up a bass amp or a kick drum, a pencil microphone to pick up something with lots of sizzle and shimmer like an acoustic guitar being strummed, or cymbals on a drum set.

Generally speaking, many dynamic (un-powered) mics have regular/mid-sized diaphragms. Condenser mics usually have either large or pencil diaphragms.

C) Tube Mics

Like condenser mics, tube mics are powered with electricity. But unlike condenser mics, tube mics do not use phantom power. Tube mics have their very own electricity-generator.

Each individual tube mic has its very own "power-supply" box. Kinda like the mic brings its own lunch to the studio - haa!

Both the tube mic and condenser mics are very sensitive, much more so than dynamic mics. This means tube and condenser mics pick up more hi-end sizzle and low-end "mmmmm" than dynamic mics.

You could say condenser and tube sound better than dynamics, but dynamic mics are better for isolating sound and they take lots more volume than tubes and condensers.

So why would you use a tube mic instead of a condenser mic or vice-versa? Well - tube mics are usually a little more delicate than condenser mics, so a condenser can take more volume than a tube mic. But, the real difference is in the tone or the character of each. Here is an example for you:

If I were to throw up a handful of sand between you and me and as the sand fell between us, I'd still be able to see you through the falling sand, but I'd see "stuff" between us. The denser sound would represent the tone of a condenser mic.

Next, I throw up some baby powder between us and as it falls I can see you, but unlike the sand, the baby powder is more transparent than the sand.

So, you could say that a tube mic has a more transparent sound, as if you can see through the sound as opposed to a condenser mic which has a "harder" sound, kinda like you can actually touch it.

Condenser Mic

>   *-Use on each instrument*
>   *In orchestra.*
>   *-Record a rapper who*
>   *Has a loud voice.*
>   *-Place six feet away from*
>   *Guitar amp.*

Tube Mic

>   *-Record an orchestra*
>   *From the audience.*
>   *-Record Celine Dion who*
>   *Has a very silky voice.*
>   *-Place across room from guitar amp.*
>   *To pick up the overall room sound.*

Microphone Pre-amp
A microphone is always plugged into a mic pre-amp. A preamp is simply an amplifier just like a guitar is plugged into a guitar amplifier.

Mic preamps come into so many shapes and colors and are made by so many different companies, but they are all the same thing - pump up the level of the microphone so the signal can be used and manipulated in your session.

A microphone generates such a tiny amount of signal on its own. Think about it: Think of a washer - you know, looks like a flat, metal donut and let's say the washer is magnetized. So now we have a washer that is a magnet. So, imagine the space in the middle of the washer - if the washer is a magnet, then you can imagine an invisible magnetic-field in the hole of the washer, kind of like a thin sheet of magnetism.

Now, take a thin nail (like a nail you would hammer into a piece of wood) and put the tip of the nail; right in the middle of the hole of the washer - the nail is in the middle, not touching any of the sides of the washer. The tip of the nail is "dipping" its toe in the middle of our magnetic lake. If there is no activity, the tip of the nail will sit there and be pulled by all the sides of the magnetic washer evenly.

But let's say I put my mouth close to the nail tip and yell. The vibration from my voice will make the tip of the nail vibrate just a lil' bit. When this happens, the nail that is suspended in this invisible lake of magnetism across the washer's hole creates a disruption in the calm magnetic field, kinda like sloshing a stick back and forth in water. This slight disruption creates a blip of electromagnetic energy and is sent to the mic-pre through the mic cable.

So now, you can imagine how tiny of a signal is generated by the nail tip vibrating in the magnetic-field of the tiny washer. It is such a minute amount of signal. This is where the mic-pre comes in.

The mic-pre receives this tiny signal and makes it louder. Think of an un-inflated balloon - it is only "so" big. But, when you blow up the balloon, it becomes like twenty times its uninflected size. Most of the " mass" of the blown-up balloon is the air blown inside it and only the outer shell is the balloon itself. I make this analogy with the balloon to illustrate the importance of the mic-pre, which is this:

The mic-pre "blows up" the tiny signal from the magnet of the microphone with electricity. So really, just like the balloon, the original signal is like the outer shell of the balloon but the majority of the size is the electricity the mic-pre pumped into the tiny signal. So, the moral of the story is:

"The better the quality of the mic-pre, the better the electricity you are puffing the signal up with. The better the electricity, the better the sound!"

It is that simple. The mic-pre one of the most important pieces in the studio.

DAW INTERFACE
As we all know, "DAW" means "Digital-Audio-Workstation." There are may different DAWS available on the market currently. Several examples are:

-Protools	-Reason
-Logic	-Ableton
-Presonus Studio 1	-Cubase
-Garage band	-Digital Performer
-FL-Studio	-etc…

To clarify, DAWS come in two parts:

1) **Software**- What you see on the screen.

2) **Hardware**-The physical piece of gear that works with the software. It is actually where you plug the microphone or instrument into. It also allows you to control the volume of the speakers and headphones usually.

The piece of hardware is also called the "Interface." Interface units commonly contain these different things:

A/D-D/A Converter - A=analog, D=digital. So, analog to digital and digital to analog. To explain, when you speak into a microphone, the signal generated by the mic is in analog form, meaning it is analogous - or the same as the original. But, to get it into the "DAW", the signal must be converted from analog into digital form. The "A/D converter" in your interface basically takes pictures of the analog signal and converts it into a series of "snapshots." Now, these digital "snapshots" are fed into the "DAW."

Once inside the "DAW," you can manipulate the sound however you choose. But in order to HEAR what you are chopping up on the screen, the digital signal must be converted from digital back to analog so it can be fed to the speakers and heard.

So really, sounds are fed from the real world into the A/D converter which allows the converted signal to be fed into the DAW. But, simultaneously ,fractions of a second later, the sound is converted back from digital to analog so we can hear what it is we just did! There sure is a lot going on in thousandths of a second.

Mic-pre(s) - Another piece of gear in the interface is a mic-pre, or multiple mic-pre's. The amount of mic-pre's in the interface is what determines how many mics you can record at the same time. If you need to use four mics on a drum set but only have two microphone inputs (mic-pre's) on your interface, guess what...you are limited to only two mics. Duh!

Many times, an engineer/producer may want to use a better quality mic-pre than is supplied by the interface. In the past, mic-pre's that come with interfaces are usually of basic quality...not bad but not the best. So many times, engineers will choose to plug the microphone into a totally separate, better quality mic-pre, then send that signal to the interface to only be converted from analog to digital by the "A/D converter" in the interface.

Speaker Volume/headphone Volume and Jack - The interface also allows you to hook speakers up to it and has a headphone jack with a separate volume control.

So you can really see that the interface of a "DAW" is like the dashboard of a car. It allows you to actually interact with the system - it is the "magic-mirror" between the real world and the digital world inside the computer.

EQUALIZERS
Equalizers are probably the most commonly-used "cosmetic" devices. By cosmetic I mean being able to change the shade or "color" of any sound. An EQ is the equivalent of a surgeon's scalpel. It is the tool that usually makes the most obvious changes to a sound, in regards to our discussion of the main tools of the trade: mic-pre's, compressors and EQ's.

Side Discussion:

Regarding "frequency," think of frequency as the higher the frequency, the higher the pitch of a note and vice-versa. To go into it a bit more we need to have a basic understanding of how sound travels through the air and how we perceive sound.

We are "swimming" through air molecules just like a fish swimming in water. It is touching and pressing on every part of the fish. We are the same way with air molecules. Thinking of one of those multi-colored ball-pits at indoor kids' playgrounds is also a good representation. When a kid jumps into the pit, the balls below his butt get pushed out of the way, which in turn bump into the balls next to them which then bump into the balls next to these and so on and so on. The balls don't necessarily move. The energy is transfered from one ball to the next, kind of like that executive toy you might see sitting on someone's desk where 5 or 6 small metal balls are hanging from what looks like fishing line and as you pull the ball on the end and let it go, it hits the second ball but then the last ball swings out on the opposite side. The energy is transfered through the middle balls, which stay stationary.

So, when someone claps their hands, the air molecules between their hands get pushed aside which bump into their neighboring air-molecules and so on all the way until the air molecules resting against your eardrums get pushed. These then push against your eardrums which then tickle nerve mechanisms inside your brain. So, to sum it all up, your eardrums get tickled which the brain picks up and then interprets as sound.

Sound is invisible but, there is a way to show it visually: This is done by what is called a "waveform." We have all seen a waveform...the squiggly, colorful patterns on the computer screen.

There are two basic ways of "measuring" sound. These are "amplitude" and "frequency."

Amplitude: Amplitude is how tall any point of the waveform is at any given spot. The taller, the louder.

Frequency: Frequency is how many times the wave "completes a cycle" in one second. Think of a wave of water. If you were in a pond of water, imagine your body completely submerged with only your head poking out of the water. Imagine that the water is right at your eye level with your nose and mouth just underneath the water surface, eyebrows above.

As you are eye-level in the water, a small rock drops into the pond and starts a wave. You would see the wave as both slightly above the water's surface, and slightly below the waters' surface. This is how a wave moves in water.

So, the water is not the wave and the wave is not the water. The wave passes through and disrupts the water. The wave and the water are two separate things all together. The wave is really invisible.

The measurement of "Hertz" is a way of measuring the "frequency" (pitch) of a sound.

1 hertz (1hz) is equal to "1 cycle per second."

It is a way of measuring sound. Thinking back to the person who is eye-level with the water in the pond, a "cycle" means one up-stroke and one down-stroke of the water-wave.

So, if three "cycles" pass at a given point in one second, that would be known as "3Hz".

So then, 50Hz would be 50 cycles (up and down waves) moving past a given point in one second.

The letter "k" is often used to mean "1,000". So,   3kHz = 3,000 hertz

AT THE END OF THE DAY...do not get caught up in trying to analyze this too much. Think of it this way:

The higher the "hertz", the higher the pitch. If referring to "equalization," the higher the hertz, the higher the "tone", or "sizzle".

Remember:

HI-END	8khz to 20khz	Treble	sizzle, ie...cymbals, saying the letter "S"
MID-RANGE	900hz to 8khz	Mids	nasal, ie...announcer at a stadium, or say "Ahh"
LOW-END	20hz to 900hz	Bass	muffled, ie...saying "Um-mmmmm"

Human hearing ranges anywhere from 20Hz (low-end) to 20KHz (hi-end). Obviously, some people don't hear as high as 20KHz and then others may hear higher than 20K.

Dogs hear past 20KHz - much closer to to 30KHz.

SIMPLE TIP:
You can think of hertz as if you say 2, 500 Hz (2.5KHz) and visualize your eardrum flapping 2,500 times in one second. There you go! Easy to visualize!

End of Side Discussion!

Back to equalization (EQ)

There are two types of equalizers common to engineers:

　　　1) Parametric
　　　2) Graphic

A parametric EQ allows you to scroll through many different frequencies as opposed to a graphic EQ which has preset frequencies.

ANOTHER MEASUREMENT OF SOUND:

1 dB = 1 Decibel

To give you an idea, the difference between the loudness of snapping your finger, and clapping is approximately 5dB or so. So you really can't hear the difference between something that is 50 dB and 51dB.

This should give you an idea, and that's good enough. At the end of the day, you'll turn a knob until it sounds good to you, and that's all that matters:)

OK - let's go back to discussing EQ. First of all, an EQ allows the user to either increase or take away whatever frequencies he chooses. To make it even simpler, let's break down what "frequencies" sound like by putting them into three categories again:

> *1) Hi's*
> *2) Mids*
> *3) Lows*

Sonic-Phonics
> **Hi's** *sound like sizzle or "sss."*
> **Mids** *sond like someone talking through a bullhorn.*
> **Lows** *sound as if someone were saying, "mmmmm."*

These three tones ("sss", "aaaah" or "mmmm") are what make up what we hear as full-range sound or, high-fidelity. These "sonic-phonics" are our hi's, mids and lows.

So, you mix: **PITCH** (frequency.... hi notes, low notes) with **VOLUME** (amplitude), and **TONE** ("sss", "aaaah", "mmm") .....and you begin to create unique sound shapes.

Question: I can hear someone asking, "Why and when would I need to 'EQ' a sound anyway?" The question is answered using a comparative question, "When and/or why would I need to salt and pepper my food?"

The answer to that is obvious. When the food is bland or not flavorful enough for us, we spice it up. This question/answer is as varied as there are individuals. Everyone is going to taste his food differently, according to his own taste.

The same goes for "seasoning" your sound. Our taste buds are much more instinctive to us, meaning, we like the taste of something or not much more clearly than whether we like the sound of something or not, so we must train our ears more so. How do we do that? A good way to train your ears is to listen to as much music as you can - expose ourselves to as much music as humanly possible.

It is equally important to listen to as many different types of music as possible, from classical to metal to electronica to country - listen to hip-hop and bluegrass to Mariachi to African Tribal. This is the very best way to condition one's ear. The more music one is exposed to, the more references one has to draw from when faced with a particular sound. It is that simple.

So, EQ-ing is as subjective and personal as beauty is. It is totally up to you. Another great way to help you "know" whether you should EQ or not is to reference your sound to a similar sound from something you like. If a snare you are recording is not making you smile when you hear it, but you don't know what is bothering you about it, play a song that you like that is somewhat similar to what it is you are working on and see what theirs sounds like. Makes it much easier.

Practice EQ-ing: Whether you are EQ-ing a single high-hat, a cluster of backround vocals at one time or EQ-ing an entire mix, practice against a reference in your spare time. What I mean is go back and forth between something out there you like, and what you are working on. Try and make yours sound like the reference...this is great practice.

There are really two steps when EQ-ing:

> 1) Find frequency you wanna add or lessen.
> 2) Add the frequency or lessen it.

With a "parametric EQ," we have many more options in terms of the specific frequencies we can play with. First, we:

1. Dial the frequency selector to whatever frequency we wanna play with
2. Then we turn the gain/reduce knob to add or lessen that frequency.

Generally speaking, parametric EQ's are used in the recording studio and graphic EQ's are many times used in live settings for "shaping" the overall sound of the P.A. system. Each night, the band plays a different arena and each arena sounds different due to whether the the walls are concrete or carpeted etc. There are a million factors that can differentiate on from the other. So, the sound guy can use a graphic EQ and "shape" the room with the sliders. If the room has too much mid-range/brightness, he can contour the room using the graphic EQ accordingly.

A graphic EQ is good for overall, general shaping where a parametric is better for specific shaping like operating a laser beam.

The Magic Frequencies - Through my many travels, I have come to the conclusion there are certain frequencies that work well on all types of sounds. From kick drums to guitars, to vocals to snare drums to violins etc...

I call these the "*Magic Frequencies*":

Add	2db of 10 KHz	adds sizzle-air
Add	1db of 6 KHz	adds definition/ diction
Add	1db of 2 KHz	attack/presence
Reduce	2db of 200 Hz	takes out mud- diness
Add	2db of 100Hz	clean, low end

If these frequencies are applied accordingly to whatever sound, the sound will take on a more defined shape. Let me describe each of these different frequencies.

1) 10K - this is like applying a bit of lip gloss. A little lip gloss on anyone makes a marked improvement in anyone's appearance. So, 10K adds a little shine, a little sprinkle to every sound.

2) 6K - adds definition to any sound; adds increased diction to any vocal performance. A little 6K will make rapper, "50-Cent" sound as if he is reciting Shakespeare.

3) 2K - this is where the attack is. 2K is that sound of the stick making contact with the snare drum; the sound of the beater of the kick drum making contact with the kick drum head. It is that "pointy" sound. Add a tad and you will bring the presence out of that sound.

By the same token, 2,000 hertz can be an annoyance and needs to be reduced from some sounds. The Jerry Lewis alter ego or maybe the actress Fran Drescher could be considered to have that whiny kind of voice. Heavy-metal guitars as well have a tendency to be very mid-rangy at times. Rolling a few decibels of 2khz out will usually soften them up a lil bit so that they are not so screechy.

4) 200Hz - 500 Hz - these frequencies tend to be really "muddy" sounding. I usually get great results by rolling a few db's of 200Hz or 250 or 300Hz etc, out of just about everything. It truly opens up most sound. Think of the frequencies between 200 - 500Hz as kind of like a beer belly. It is not really attractive on anyone.

The only time I may add 200Hz to an instrument might be if a Tom Tom is missing the "bounce," of the "doooom" sound characteristic to Tom Toms. This is the only time when these frequencies seem to help.

5) 90-130Hz - this frequency range is really clean, open and low end. Like a great butt, it is round just in the right places and invisible in just the right places. What more can I say?!

Hardware vs. Plugins:

I am asked all the time whether using an actual compressor that is bolted into a rack is better that its virtual counterparts or vice versa. This is a great question. Before giving an answer, let's explore how it is that this came to be.

Obviously, there were no "virtual" compressor, EQ's or anything else before let's say the year 2000. Since audio recording began to evolve in sophistication around the 1940's or so, compressors and EQ's were actual hard devices. Not until DAW's (digital audio workstations, ie: Protools, Reason, etc.) did virtual versions of compressors, EQ's, Reverbs etc. appear.

At first, when virtual plugins began to come out, there were not a lot to choose from. Some were quite good and some were just absolutely awful. Software makers like effects-plug-ins company "Waves" were pioneers in creating virtual versions of classic "hard" devices. There are many companies and an abundance of virtual plugins available now.

Regarding whether a particular hard device or its virtual counterpart is "better" is a subjective question. Both have their pros and cons. The older hard devices get more idiosyncratic the older they become. Years of wear and tear make gear perform differently. Some studios will "endure" heavy cigarette smoke, others heavy weed smoke. Some gear has had liquid spilled on it while others have been literally dropped on the ground by accident. So, an "LA - 2A" compressor in one studio will more than likely have a different sound/feel than an identical "LA - 2A" in a different studio. So when you find a really sweet sounding one, you get spoiled. You go to another room and it is not as sweet. It is much more brittle sounding.

On the other hand, virtual plugins always stay consistent from one computer to another. An "LA - 2A" on one computer will sound exactly like an "LA - 2A" on another rig. Also, the virtual devices will recall exactly the same settings you had every time you open the session as opposed to a hard unit which will always be just a little off even in the best scenario.

Virtual outboard gear (plugins) also can be made to "glitch-out" on purpose. By over-tweaking" the controls on some virtual devices, the gear will do unexpected things which the authors of the software had never intended. One very popular example of this is the "auto-tune" sound. The "robotic" sound is actually the device freaking out...over-processing. But, serendipitiously, it sounds unique. The first popular example of this was heard on Cher's 90's hit, "Do You Believe In Love After Love?" Artist T-Pain then wore the auto-tune sound into the ground during the mid 2000's.

So, in conclusion, hard devices tend to have individual personality as virtual versions have uniformity and the ability to be "glitched-out."

COMPRESSORS

Compressors are very curious devices...probably the most misunderstood devices in a studio.

Nowadays we have "plug-ins," meaning virtual effect boxes of every kind in every DAW, (digital audio work station). Plug-ins are much easier to use than their real world counterparts (meaning actual, physical compressors, reverbs etc found in racks at studios). Plug-ins are easier to use because most of them are pre-set to a default setting so that when you first mount the plug-in to a channel in your system, the plug-in pretty much does what it is intended to do, especially utility devices like compressors.

What I am aim to do first in this discussion of compressors is give the user a firm understanding of what compressors and limiters are usually used for, what the basic knobs do on a compressor and then most importantly, how to apply a compressor to your life/music and make people's heads nod up and down. Without practical application, it's all just a bunch of theoretical rhetoric.

To begin, let's make a distinction between a compressor and a limiter. Think of a compressor as a lazy limiter, or a limiter as a compressor on sterroids. More on this later.

I like to keep things simple, so I will break it down in a very simplified way.

So, to keep it simple, first think to yourself, "Do I want to protect or destroy a sound?" "WHAT?!" I can hear people saying, "protect or destroy?!" Think of it this way - a sound we might want to "protect" might be a VOCAL, and a sound we might want to "destroy" or "obliterate" might be a snare drum sound.

Imagine this...look at a door near you, any door. If you were to throw a piece of fruit at the door, you would hear a "pop" as the fruit smashed into the door. Think of this as destroying a sound.

Now, imagine you had the power to turn the door into a wall of cotton-balls. If you were to throw another piece of fruit at this soft wall, when the fruit would hit the wall of cotton-balls, it would sink into the wall and then drop softly to the floor un-smashed and fully intact. The wall of cotton-balls would protect the fruit instead of demolishing it the way the hard surface did.

So, from these examples, if we were about to record a drum set and the snare drum does not have the "pop" we want, we can insert a compressor between the microphone and the recorder (really between the mic-pre and the re-corder) so the snare collides as if into a brick wall and gets splattered by the compressor. It will create more of a "pop" like the fruit thrown at a door.

At the other end of the spectrum, if we are about to record a lead vocal, we don't want the vocal to distort by arriving at the recording device at too hot a level. In order to prevent this potential distortion, we again place a compressor between the mic-pre and the recorder and set the compressor so it acts like a wall of cotton-balls protecting the vocal from "hurting its head". Think of a gymnast on a trampoline jumping so high that she hits her head on the ceiling above.

These are just two basic examples. Obviously in the real world there are an infinite amount of scenarios. We are discussing two very opposing scenarios to show the extreme contrast and wide range of possible uses of compressors.

So, next let's discuss how to turn a compressor into either a "hard" or "soft" surface. There are two controls pretty universal to most compressors: "Threshold" and "Ratio/Compression." To understand what these knobs do, let's again use an analogy.

Let's think of a racquet-ball court. A racquet-ball court has a ceiling that is part of the court meaning that if the ball hits the ceiling, the ball is still in play. So, the ceiling is part of the playable court. Imagine there is a huge cranking lever just outside the court where we can raise the height of the ceiling 30 feet into the air or lower the ceiling so low that we would have to play raquet-ball on our knees. We can raise or lower the ceiling either up or down. This is "threshold."

Side note...
We live in a world where we turn knobs from left to right to get more...left to right to get more volume, left to right to get more more heat, left to right to get more water etc.

The crazy thing about the threshold knob is that it is backwards. One would think that when you turn the threshold "up" (to the right), you are "adding more" of it to the sound. Not true with threshold. You turn the threshold knob right to left to "add more." Let's explore.

Think of the threshold knob again as being able to either raise or lower the ceiling of a racquet-ball court. Think that if the knob is on "10," meaning the knob is all the way to the right, then the ceiling of the racquet-ball court

61

is on the "tenth-floor" as opposed to the knob's being on "1" which would mean that the knob is on the "first-floor."

If the ceiling were on the "first-floor", there would be much more of a chance that the ball would hit the ceiling as opposed to it's being on the "tenth-floor" where the ceiling would be much higher. If the ceiling is really high, the ball (representing the sound) will not hit the ceiling as much as it would if it were low, therefore the ball is not affected by the ceiling as much.

But, this is only half of the equation. Let's now talk about the other common knob on the compressor: "Ratio/compression."

Ratio/compression - The "Ratio" knob is sometimes labeled "compression" and vice-versa. In essence, they mean the same thing. To make another simple analogy, if the threshold knob controls how high or low the ceiling of the racquet-ball court is, the ratio/compression knob controls what the ceiling is made of. We can choose to make it as soft as a ceiling made out of cotton balls, or as hard as steel. Think of it this way: the lower the ratio, the softer the ceiling.

> *1:1 Cotton balls*
> *2:1 Pillows*
> *3:1 Rubber*
> *4:1 Cardboard*
> *5:1 Balsa-wood/styrofoam*
> *6:1 Wood*
> *7:1 Concrete*
> *etc...*

(Compressor radio-knobs allow you to choose from 1:1 and on up, as opposed to the ratio knob on a limiter which start at 10:1 or 20:1 and go up.)

To sum things up about compressors, here is a simple way to go about applying them:

1. See if there are any sounds in your production that need either more "pop", or need to be "softened up". For example, a snare drum often needs more "pop", and a vocal often needs to be softened up, especially if the singer gets really loud at spots in the song.

2. Insert the compressor of your choice on the track/sound you want to either smash, or soften up.

3. Immediately, set the ratio to 3:1, and turn the threshold all the way up to the right (if it is a knob), or all the way up (if a vertical slider). A 3:1 ratio is a good medium-strength ceiling hardness to start at. Not too hard, not too soft.

4. Next, put the track with the compressor on it in "solo" mode so you will be able to hear how you are affecting the sound.

5. Now, begin to lower the Threshold slider or knob slowly until you see the "GR" (gain-reduction) light/meter begin to blink. When this happens, it means you have lowered the ceiling of the "gym" down to where the "gymnast's" head is touching the ceiling each time she jumps up.

6. From here, use your ears. What do you want to achieve? Do you want to smash the sound?...then lower the Threshold even lower until you like what you hear. If you want to protect a vocal sound from spiking too high, back the Ratio down to maybe 2:1, and lower the Threshold just a lil bit to keep the loud notes from hitting their head too hard on the ceiling.

THERE IS NO RIGHT OR WRONG WAY TO USE A COMPRESSOR.
As long as you have an idea of what it can do, it is up to you to be creative with it and make it do whatever you like:)

PART THREE

Mic Placement for Recording Instruments and Vocals

Mic placement is not an exact science! There is no right or wrong way to place a microphone on an instrument.

The main rule-of-thumb is to take a moment to actually listen to the sound you are wanting to record. Many people will just grab any 'ol mic and set it up without really listening to the sound.

Take a moment and just listen. Ask yourself:

*Where is the most sound coming from?

*Do I want the echo of the room, or just the close, dry sound of the instrument itself?

*Is it a loud sound coming from an amp or is it a quiet sound as if someone were whispering?

*Do I need to use more than one mic at the same time in order to record multiple instruments simultaneously, as if mixing up a drum set?

Generally speaking, if you were to record something very loud, you should probably use a dynamic microphone. If you need to record multiple instruments that are close together such as a snare, tom tom, hihat, etc., you should probably use dynamic mics so each mic only picks up the drum that is being miked and not the neighboring drums.

If you are recording something that is not amplified, you then should probably use a condenser mic to pick up all details of the sound. This list includes:

-vocals
-violin
-piano
-acoustic guitar
-guitar amp - six feet away from amp
-bass amp - three feet away from amp

-entire drum kit - in middle of room to capture the ambiance of the room.

Mic Placement Examples

1) Guitar

Electric guitar (amp) - place a dynamic mic right up against the screen covering the speaker. Remember, dynamic mics can take very loud volumes.

Also, maybe place a condenser mic about six feet or more away from the speaker to capture the ambiance of the room echo.

Acoustic guitar - place a condenser mic near the sound-hole, maybe nine inches to one foot away. To assure you have the very best spot, ask the guitarist to play as you place your ear close to the sound-hole. Move your ear around the sound-hole area to find the very best sounding spot.

2) Bass

Bass guitars are recorded two different ways:

> *A) mic on the amp speaker*
> *B) using a "Direct Box."*

First, it is wise to use a large-diaphragm dynamic mic on a bass speaker. Bass sound waves are much wider apart, so - the bigger the pick-up area of the mic, the better the bass sound you will capture.

My favorite large-diaphragm dynamic mic is the AKG-D112. It sounds great on bass amps and kick drums as well. Place the mic three inches or so away from the bass amp speaker.

Also, try placing a condenser mic three to six feet away from the bass-amp speaker in order to capture the ambient room echo from the bass amp. When blending the close, dynamic mic sound with the condenser mic sound, you get a really great, full-bodied sound.

Using a "Direct-Box" on the bass

A Direct-Box is really just an adaptor, meaning it allows for connecting a guitar cable (¼ inch jack) to a microphone cable. (XLR).

So, what you do instead of plugging the bass guitar directly into the bass amp head, you plug the bass guitar into the Direct-Box.

Then, on the other side of the Direct-Box there are two empty jacks. One is to connect to the bass amp head and the other jack is an "XLR" jack which you plug directly into a microphone pre-amp.

Now you have a microphone on the bass amp speaker that picks up the sound of the amp and you also have the Direct-Box plugged in to pick up the sound of the bass guitar itself.

You will record the 'mic" and the "Direct" signals on two separate tracks so you have total control over each when you are ready to mix it all down.

3) Drums

Recording a drum set is both challenging and fun. It is an art form in and of itself. I absolutely love the challenge because every drum-set is a unique collection and configuration of drums.

Take your time when mixing up a drum kit. If you have the time, allocate at least a few hours to mic up and get the sound right.

Again, there is no right or wrong way way to mic up drums, but I will give you some basic steps to follow that I know you will have great results with.

Let's break the entire process down into several steps:

* Choosing all the mics for each drum
* Physically setting mics on stands and wiring
* Placing each mic to each drum
* Plugging each mic into a mic-pre
* Getting actual mic sounds
* Adjusting microphone positioning on each drum

Choosing the right mic for each drum is a personal choice... again, there is no right or wrong way. I will however suggest some mics that work great for me.

Snare drum - Shure SM-57 positioned about three to five inches above the snare head placed at a diagonal angle to the snare.

Do not put the mic too close to the snare - you will get a much richer and pure tone if you allow a bit of space between the mic and snare head. You can also put a second dynamic mic aimed at the bottom head of the snare to pick up more "rattle." Beware of "phasing which is described just below.

Kick-drum - AKG-D112 just at the hole in the front of the kick. When I say "front," I mean the side of the kick drum the audience sees. The D-112 (large-diaphragm dynamic mic) will give you the "thump" sound which is the heart of your kick drum tone.

You can also add a large condenser mic one to three feet from the kick drum. This will give you a nice, open, roomy sound when added to the thump of the D-112 in the hole.

Side Note...
PHASING - Sometimes when you have two mics picking up the same sound, you may encounter the mics being "out of phase." This is when both mics "cancel" each other out and instead of creating a bigger sound together, they create a nasty, thin sound together.

This can be fixed by either hitting the "phase switch" on the mic-pre (which has a zero with a diagonal line through it), or can be fixed by simply moving one of the mics away from the other just a 'lil bit.

ok...back to miking...

Hi-Hat - use any pencil or regular diaphram dynamic mic for the Hi-Hat. Aim it about four to five inches above the top of the Hi-Hat. Make sure to position the mic to the Hi-Hat with the Hi-Hat in the open position. If you place the mic with the pedal depressed, the Hi-Hat may hit the mic when the drumer opens Hi-Hat during recording.

Toms - a great mic for Toms is the Sennheiser 421. They are great on Toms because they have a bigger diaphragm than a standard dynamic mic and pick up better "lows". Toms have lots of low end.

Cymbals - using condenser mics overhead always works well. Place one mic about six feet above the Hi-Hat and the other about six feet above the floor tom. Point both mics so they are pointing at the drummer's head.

These two mics are sent to two separate tracks in your recorder. On your mixer, "pan" the condenser mic above the Hi-Hat all the way to the left and the other mic over the floor tom all the way to the right. This will give you a cool "stereo-effect" - a really nice, spacial sound.

Room mics - you can have fun with room mic choice and placement. Any condenser or tube mic will work. If you have some mics left over, try experimenting with different combinations of room mics. You can use one, two, three or even four mics placed in different parts of the room to capture so many cool, unique combinations of sound. The sky is the limit in capturing "room sounds."

John Bonham drum sound from Led Zepplin optimizes a great "room sound." Guitarist Jimmy Page produced Led Zepplin and recorded the drums in a castle. Castles usually have thick stone walls which reflect sound and adds a certain warm tone to the sound. So the surfaces of the walls in your recording room play a big part in the overall sound you get.

If you are working in a room that has surfaces that reflect lots of sound, (hard surfaces like concrete, wood, stone, etc,), you can "tighten" up your room sound by hanging up some blankets on the walls. Be creative. The ticker the material you hang, the more sound will be absorbed. Be ghetto and tape blankets to the walls if you have to!

On the other hand, if your room is real dead sounding because you have carpet in the walls, you can liven up the room by leaning sheets of wood against the walls. Again, be creative! There is no right way or wrong way to get a unique sound.

Recording Vocals
When recording vocals, try to put you vocalist in as small and as tight-sounding of a room as possible. If you have to, tape blankets to the walls of a closet or bathroom to create a tight sound. Nowhere is it written that a bathroom cannot be an effective vocal booth.

A decent, large-diaphragm condenser mic will sound great for vocals, regardless of the vocal style.

It is very important to use a "popper-stopper: between the mic and the vocalist. The four-fingers measuring method is a reliable way to figure how much distance there should be between the mic and the popper-stopper.

You should be able to put four fingers (imagine a karate-chop) between the mic and the popper-stopper.

Re-amping - reamping is a great way to turn a mundane sound into something really cool. Let's say you have a keyboard sound recorded from one of the virtual synths in your DAW. It sounds cool but you are not jumping up and down.

Re-amping is running that bland keyboard sound out of the computer using a guitar cable into another room and plugging the other end into an actual guitar amp. Once this sound is playing out of the guitar amp, you then put a mic (or combination of mics) on the amp and then record it on another track back into your DAW!

This is so much fun because the room the amp is in creates the ambiance and is picked up by the mics. So now that bland keyboard sound has a live feel. Try it on everything. It works great.

Introduction to Digital Audio Workstations (DAWs)

First of all, let me be the first one to say that the acronym "DAW" is corny-sounding....daw daw daw....sounds silly to say, kind of like you don't know what to say like "DUH!", but for simplicity sake, we'll use it.

There are many different daws made by many different companies on the market as of 2011. The good news is that they all basically do the same things:

-record sound
-allow you to move the sounds around
-allow you to shape the sound using tools like equalizers, reverbs, compressors and so many others
-allow you to blend all the separate sounds together (final mix) then "burn" (record) the mix to a cd, dvd or hard-drive.

All the different DAWs on the market are kind of like all the different types of cars there are...so many different shapes, sizes from luxury to economy... but they all do the same basic things:

-drive
-turn left or right
-stop
-back up

If you know the gas pedal, brake pedal, and steering-wheel, you can drive pretty much any vehicle whether it be a go-cart to a 18-wheeler.

The same goes for daws. If you understand the basics of:

-record (get sounds in the box)
-edit (move sounds around if you need to)
-playback (listen to what you captured and altered)

If you understand these basics, you can pretty much jump on any daw and understand it without too much difficulty. You just have to make yourself familiar with where the" tools" are (gas-pedal, brake-pedal, steering-wheel) in each different daw.

Me personally, I don't pick up and absorb new technology as fast as the other guy, but once I get used to something, I can learn to pop better wheelies than anyone on the track. Haa!

Some people enjoy learning all types of new technology and software all the time which is really cool...not me. I learn new software on a need-to basis... haa. I'd rather get really, really great at one system than rather be just OK on many. If you pick up new technology easily, GREAT!...you have an advantage. It all depends on who you are trying to become.

If your goal is to operate gear and be more of an engineer (which I was for 15 years before daws ever came out), then you might wanna learn a few different daws so you can work with many different clients. If you want to produce your own music, you might wanna focus in on one or two different daws and get really good at one of them so the technology and tools don't slow up your creative-process.

There is nothing worse than having a great idea for a song...it is in your head...you hear the whole thing done in your head, but you only know your system a lil bit, so you are not able to express/lay-down the creative idea the way you hear it...it does not translate into the box like you hear it in your head!! That SUCKS!!

But when you understand the technology like the back of your hand, you don't even have to think about the technology and can focus only on getting what's in your head into the box exactly as you hear it. I'm tellin' you....this is the truth!! This is the difference between just laying your stuff down, or truly crafting something.

PRESONUS "STUDIO 1" DAW

PreSonus is a fast-growing audio gear company. Recently, it put out a new DAW called "Studio 1".

I know if I show someone where the "gas-pedal, brake-pedal and steering-wheel" is, they have enough information to start learning how to drive. It is up to them to go further if they like. Like anything, the more you practice, the better you get...PERIOD.

I also know that if you try and absorb too much trivial at first, it will only slow you down...kind of like showing you how the electrical-system of the car is wired and requiring you to memorize it before you know how to use the gas, brake, and steering-wheel!

So let's get you started with PreSonus Studio 1.

FIRST OF COURSE, IT HAS TO BE 'INSTALLED" ON YOUR COMPUTER. Duh. THIS IS A PRETTY SIMPLE THING TO DO.

1. IF YOU HAVE A PRESONUS STUDIO 1 INSTALL DISC, JUST POP IT IN AND FOLLOW THE INSTRUCTIONS.

2. IF YOU ARE DOWNLOADING STUDIO 1 FROM THE PRESONUS WEB-SITE, FOLLOW THE STEP BY STEP INSTRUCTIONS AND MAKE SURE YOU HAVE A "SERIAL NUMBER" THAT SHOULD HAVE BEEN SUPPLIED TO YOU BY EITHER CAMP-JAM OR PRE-SONUS.

Either way, you will have to set up a user account with presonus which is simple to do...just go to their website: PreSonus.com

DIFFERENT WINDOWS IN S1
(We'll call the "Studio 1" program "S1" from here on.)

The main window S1 defaults to is called the "arrange" window. This window allows you to see audio waveforms from left to right.

Another useful window in S1 is the "console" window. Go to "view" at the top bar and click on "console".

A new window will pop open on the bottom half of the arrange window.

Here you see:

> -faders (volume up and down)
> -the panner just above (left or right speaker)
> -"M" for mute (turn off) and "S" for solo (hear only this track)

At the top of the track looking at the "console" there is a dark area.

> -The top line is the "INPUT"
> -The bottom line is the "OUTPUT"

The output should be defaulted to "MAIN OUT" already, so really only the input must be adjusted.

If you plug a instrument or mic into hole #2 on the interface unit, then you need to assign the track's INPUT to "input 2".

OPEN A NEW "SESSION"

I say "new" session meaning I want to start a new song from scratch. The term "session" basically means song...it is easier if you think of it this way at first.

In S1, the word "song" is used instead of "session"...that's cool of them.

On the opening page once you "launch" the program, you have the option at the top to either:

> *1. "Create a new song"*
> *or*
> *2. "Open an existing song"*

Obviously, if you have been working on a particular song in the past in s1 and you wanna do more work on the song, then you'd click on #2..."open an existing song".

Let's stick right now with getting set up to create a new song.

1. Launch S1. Find it in your dock or wherever your programs are stored in your computer.

2. Click on "create a new song" tab at top left of screen that pops up.

3. This window will open and give you many options:

> a. the first option on the left "empty song" should be high-lighted. Leave it there.
>
> b. on the right side of the open window, it says "song title" Make sure to name the song something you'll remember later.
>
> c. the options below (sample rate, resolution, timebase, song length) are fine. Leave them as they are.
>
> d. click "OK" at bottom right

TIME TO OPEN SOME NEW TRACKS.

Think of tracks as lanes on a highway. They all run side by side. Tracks are where each different instrument is recorded to.

There are a few different types of tracks, but the ones we need to focus on right now are:

> 1. *audio tracks*
>
> 2. *instrument tracks*

Audio tracks actually hold real recorded sound, as opposed to Instrument tracks which record only MIDI information. What does this mean, you say? You can think of MIDI info as you only tapping a key on a keyboard but not recording the sound it makes. If you play the 19th white key on a midi keyboard, only the push of the key is recorded, not any sound is recorded. The computer remembers that only the 19th white key was pressed at that given moment.

The other part of this whole equation of course is the sound, of course. So now that you have some keys to press, you need something to generate a sound. This is where Virtual Synths come into play.

What is a virtual synth? It is the brains of a synthesizer simulated in a computer program. It is one of the coolest things to ever happen to music recording. So...the keyboard "triggers" whatever sound the virtual synth is set to.

BACK TO OPENING UP NEW TRACKS...

First, open up a new track by going to the top menu bar and:

1. Click on "track"

2. Go down to the second option "add audio track (mono)"

3. Make sure the track input matches the hole you are going to plug into on the interface

For recording actual sounds like guitars and voices, plug your instrument or microphone into the Interface. Remember, the interface is the device that translates actual sound into digital info so the computer can store/record it.

Remember, the hole on the interface must match the track-input you are intending to record onto.

4. Next, while looking at the "arrange" window, make the track "record-ready" by clicking on the circle just below the "M" mute button.

Turn the corresponding knob up you are plugged into on the interface while you talk into the mic or play your instrument.

Keep turning the knob up on the interface until you get a good signal on the track meter. A good signal means the light meter should almost hit the top.

BEGIN RECORDING

Next we need to make the car "go".

To make s1 play, either press the space bar or click on the sideways triangle at the very bottom of the screen.

To make s1 stop, either hit the space bar again, or click on the square nest to the sideways triangle.

To make s1 record, either hit the * (asterisk) symbol on the far right of the keypad, or click on the circle also next to the sideways triangle at the very bottom of the screen.

Tap the "minus" symbol on the very far right side of your keyboard a few times to make the play cursor begin at the beginning (all the way to the left border).

You might want to set a tempo for your idea by using the metronome/click in S1

1. on top menu line, click on "transport"
2. all the way down it says "metronome setup"
3. make sure "click in play" is checked
4. now go to very bottom of S1 screen...just to the right of the center, you'll see "metronome".
5. make sure the little triangle-arrow pointing down to the right just above the word is lit. This will allow you to hear the clicks when you hit play.
6. to the right of "metronome" at bottom of screen is "tempo".
7. to change the tempo, while in play, simply hold down the mouse on the number above the word "tempo" and physically move the mouse up to speed up the tempo, or drag mouse down to slow tempo. Drag to wherever tempo feels good to you.

MIXING

The art of mixing a song is an entire process in itself. Basically, once you have all the sounds recorded, you then need to make sure all of the levels are playing together beautifully without anything jumping out too loud, or any sound too quiet to be heard.

A good way to begin the mixing process is to pull all of the faders on the console screen all the way down.

On the console screen, the channel all the way to the right that says "Main Out" at the bottom is your "master-fader". It is kind of like your speedometer on your car. You wanna keep your eye on this guy to make sure the overall signal is not hitting all the way up to the top. If it does, you'll probably get unwanted distortion on your CD when you burn it.

Then first:

1. push the kick drum track up until it makes the master fader hit at about -12 on the meter.

2. now bring up the next drum sound so it plays well with the kick drum.

3. continue to bring each instrument up one by one. Listen to each instrument as you bring it up...see if you can hear the new sound as well as the one you brought it up against. As you continue to do this, the mix will begin to blossom.

4. step away from the mix periodically to keep a clear mind. Sitting too long listening to the same sounds over and over can make you lose your overall clarity.